The Russian Army of the Napoleonic Wars

Albert Seaton • Illustrated by Michael Youens

Series editor Martin Windrow

First published in the United States 1973

ISBN 0 88254 167 6

First published in Great Britain in 1973 by
Osprey Publishing, Elms Court, Chapel Way,
Botley, Oxford OX2 9LP, United Kingdom.
Email: info@ospreypublishing.com

Reprinted 2002, 2005

In the preparation of this text acknowledgement is
made to *Opisanie Odezhdui Vooruzheniya Rossiiskikh
Voisk* edited by Viskovatov (St Petersburg 1899–
1902) and *L'Armée Russe* by Bujac (Paris 1894). The
photographs are reproduced by courtesy of the
Keeper, the Library of the Victoria and Albert
Museum (Photographer: Berkhamsted Photographic,
Berkhamsted, Hertfordshire). Grateful acknowledgement is made to Macmillan Ltd. for permission to
reproduce extracts from the accounts of Sir Robert
Wilson and Sir Robert Porter, included in *1812*
edited by Anthony Brett-James.

CIP Data for this publication is available from the
British Library

Printed in China through World Print Ltd.

FOR A CATALOGUE OF ALL BOOKS PUBLISHED
BY OSPREY PLEASE CONTACT:

NORTH AMERICA
Osprey Direct, 2427 Bond Street,
University Park, IL 60466, USA
E-mail: info@ospreydirectusa.com

ALL OTHER REGIONS
Osprey Direct UK, P.O. Box 140, Wellingborough,
Northants, NN8 2FA, UK
E-mail: info@ospreydirect.co.uk

www.ospreypublishing.com

Introduction

Until the end of the sixteenth century there was no standing army in times of peace in Russia. When danger threatened or a campaign was to be mounted, the ruler ordered the nobility into the field and these armed and provisioned their own retainers and serfs. In consequence there was no uniformity in organization, equipment, or dress; nor was the Principality of Moscow militarily strong enough to withstand invading armies, whether from out of Asia or out of Europe.

Muscovy survived because of its privileged position among the Russian principalities as the tax-gatherer for the overlord Tartar, who held dominion over the Slav lands as far west as the Dnieper. The Mongol-Tartar Empire began rapidly to decline with the separation of the Golden Horde from the Mongols, while in the west the Tartars were challenged by the growing military power of Lithuania-Poland. It was Ivan III who first threw off the Tartar yoke, but by then the Golden Horde was breaking up into the three separate Tartar khanates of the Crimea, Kazan, and Astrakhan. Not until the accession of Ivan IV (the Terrible) was the first body of Muscovite troops set up as a permanent establishment in peace. This was the corps of *streltsy*, the *strelets* being an archer or musketeer usually recruited from the peasantry. The *streltsy* lived in barracks and garrisoned Moscow and the frontier towns, being responsible not only for defence but for police, fire and watch duties.

The original *streltsy* organization was that of the company and it was not until the mid-seventeenth century that the many independent companies were united into regiments. In all there were forty regiments, each about 600 strong, the men-at-arms carrying a sword, an axe, and a musket or pike.

The use of artillery field-pieces had first been introduced in 1389, but it was not until 1550 that a permanent artillery force came into being. Artillerymen, however, like those elsewhere in western Europe, were not regarded as soldiers but merely as camp-following auxiliaries.

The reign of Boris Godunov and the 'Time of the Troubles' showed that the *streltsy* was little more than a territorial militia unfit for European war. Large numbers of mercenary soldiers flocked to offer their services to Moscow – Germans, Livonians, and Swedes predominant among them,

A grenadier of the Preobrazhensky Regiment, *c*. 1801

and these formed the officer and non-commissioned officer cadres for newly-raised cavalry, dragoon, and infantry regiments, organized and equipped on the Western pattern. Of the regiments founded in 1642, the Moskovsky continued in service until 1792, and the Butirsky, under its changed title of 13 Erivansky Grenadiers, until 1917. When Peter the Great came to the throne in 1689, his predecessor Theodor had left him a standing army of twenty-five regiments of cavalry and forty regiments of infantry.

Peter the Great

Peter the Great in his youth had played at soldiers, drilling and exercising his two companies of the Preobrazhensky and the Semenovsky. In 1689 and 1691 these two names were transferred to two of his newly formed guard regiments, while the cannoniers of his childhood were formed into the 1st Battery of the Artillery Brigade of the Guard.

In 1697 Peter left on a tour of western Europe and during his absence the *streltsy* mutinied, possibly incited to do so by Peter's sister Sophia, the former Regent. The *streltsy* were already a political power within the state and to this they owed their bloody suppression on the Tsar's return. Their remnants were disbanded and Peter determined that many of the foreign mercenary regiments should be abolished, their replacements being found by a national conscription introduced in 1699. Only a proportion of the male population was called to the colours for an unlimited period of full-time service, which really meant for life. (Not until fifty years later was the term of service regulated to twenty-five years, this law, enacted by the Empress Anne, remaining in force until 1874.)

Peter's first conscription brought him only 32,000 recruits and these, drafted into twenty-seven infantry and two dragoon regiments, were formed into three infantry divisions under the command of Weide, Repnin, and Galovin. But Peter could not, and probably would not, rid himself of the foreign officers on whom he relied for experience and instruction, for of the twenty-seven infantry regiments, twenty-two were commanded by colonels with German names, while four of the remaining five had non-Russian names. The two colonels of dragoons were called Schneewanz and Goltz, Goltz's regiment still being in existence in 1917 as 1 Moskovsky Dragoons. In 1708 most of the original twenty-nine regiments were given titles of the names of towns or provinces, usually where they were raised, and many of these were retained until the twentieth century. The only Imperial Tsarist Russian regiments which could claim existence before this time were certain cavalry who owed their earliest origins to the 'town Cossack' levies of South-west Muscovy and the Ukraine, the Sumsky, Kharkovsky, Izyumsky, Akhtirsky, and the Chernigovsky, Seversky, and Kievsky regiments.

In 1700 the new Russian Army was completely defeated by Charles XII of Sweden on the Narva, with only the regiments of the Russian guard showing any great steadiness. Undeterred, the Tsar reorganized his forces, but continued to place his trust in his infantry rather than in

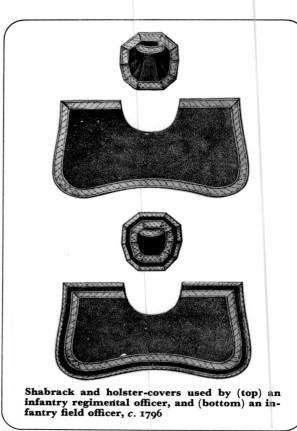

Shabrack and holster-covers used by (top) an infantry regimental officer, and (bottom) an infantry field officer, c. 1796

4

artillery or mounted troops. By 1709, when the Swedes were defeated by Peter at Poltava in the Ukraine, the strength of the Russian Army had risen to 90,000 men, with fifty-three regiments of infantry of the line and thirty-two of mounted infantry dragoons. It had no light or heavy cavalry.

In 1720 Peter the Great reformed his army once more and the effect of these changes was still apparent seventy years later at the time of the Napoleonic Wars.

The overall army strength was increased to 125,000 men, half of which were allocated to field formations, the remainder providing garrison troops and static installations. And so there were forty-eight regiments of field and forty-eight of garrison infantry; each regiment had two battalions, each of four companies of musketeers, together with a ninth (regimental) company of grenadiers. A battalion was about 600 men strong and four battalions (two regiments) formed a corps.

The mounted force numbered 40,000 of which 36,000 served in the field force. The whole of the regular cavalry of forty-one regiments were of dragoons, each regiment consisting of ten companies of mounted infantry and one of mounted grenadiers.

Hussars formed no part of the army after 1707, the place of light cavalry being filled by mounted Cossacks of the main hosts. There were originally two types of Cossack: the 'town Cossacks', permanent bodies of troops raised by frontier Russian towns, these eventually being absorbed into the regular cavalry; and the Cossacks of the hosts (*voiska*) of the Don, the Terek, the Ural, and Siberia. These were warrior settler peoples who were obliged to provide the Tsar with mounted troops in exchange for certain freedoms from taxation and for the grant of common rights and lands. Each Cossack from the hosts was responsible for furnishing, at his own expense, his horse, uniform, arms and equipment. Cossack ranks, methods and training were very different from those of the regular army and, with his scant regard for formal discipline, the Cossack was viewed by his Russian brother as more than unreliable.

The artillery arm was still little developed

Grenadiers of the Preobrazhensky, Semenovsky, and Izmailovsky Guard Regiments, c. 1797

although it had taken under its wing the engineers, the sappers, and the miners. An artillery regiment might have as many as 11,000 men on its strength, including six companies of cannoniers (guns), a company of bombardiers (originally mortars and howitzers), and several companies of miners and pontoniers. This was -additional to what was known as 'battle artillery', the light guns belonging to infantry and cavalry regiments, for each line regiment had three cannon or mortars under its own command, and the Preobrazhensky and Semenovsky Guards each had ten.

Early Eighteenth-Century Changes

Peter the Great died in 1725 and, if one excepts the forming (in 1728) of a new engineer corps independent of the artillery, there were no further changes until the accession of the Empress Anne in 1730. That year a new guards infantry regiment

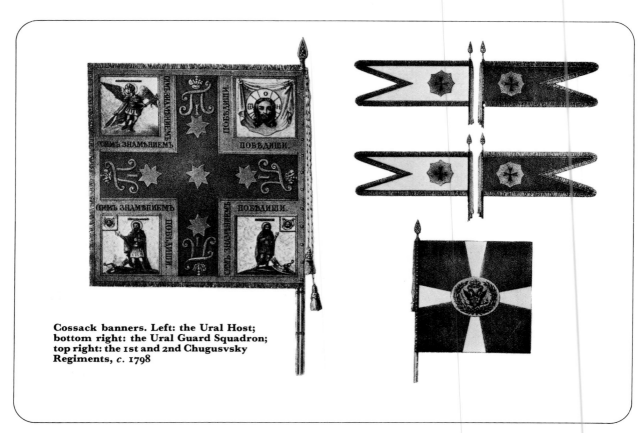

Cossack banners. Left: the Ural Host; bottom right: the Ural Guard Squadron; top right: the 1st and 2nd Chugusvsky Regiments, *c.* 1798

was raised, the Izmailovsky, and a number of dragoon regiments were reformed as the Imperial Horse Guards.

The Russian mounted arm had had very little success against the Turkish light cavalry. The Cossack was valueless for shock action against enemy horse, and the Russian dragoon was better trained as an infantry soldier than as a cavalryman. The native Russian horse lacked weight, bone and stamina compared with the Turkish-bred Arab. It was only at the prompting of the Russian Field-Marshal Münnich that the Empress Anne agreed to the formation of three regiments of heavy cuirassiers, equipped with a metal helmet and breastplate and mounted on well-bred horses imported from Germany. An attempt was made, too, to reform the Cossacks and use at least part of their number as cavalry by regrouping many of their independent squadrons (*sotni* or hundreds) into regiments.

It was during Anne's reign, too, that the infantry grenadier changed his basic function (although he retained his name) and became a musketeer-infantryman, grenade-throwing being an additional, specialized skill. Nor were fusiliers necessarily armed with the fusil or light musket.

The value of Russian troops was still an unknown factor in Europe, for, although Peter had overcome the Swedes at Poltava, within two years he suffered a near-disastrous defeat at the hands of the Turks on the Pruth. Anne intervened in the War of the Polish Succession and fought another war against the Turks, this time in company with Austria as a Russian ally. But Russian successes were comparatively trifling and it was left to the Empress Elisabeth (1741–62) to pit her armies against a European foe.

In 1753 the Russian line infantry regiments were reformed from a two- to a three-battalion structure, each having three companies of fusiliers and one of grenadiers. Grenadier regiments on the other hand remained on a two-battalion organization with an additional company to each battalion, making ten companies to the regiment. Garrison regiments of infantry remained at two battalions each.

Russian cavalry, too, was reorganized, and between 1741 and 1759 twelve new hussar

Cavalry helmets, 1799

regiments were raised, the ranks being filled for the most part by light cavalry enlisted from abroad. In 1756 nine existing Russian dragoon regiments were re-formed as nine cuirassier regiments and six regiments of horse grenadiers. Most mounted regiments had an establishment of five squadrons, but the dragoons had six and the hussars had a loose company (half-squadron) organization which varied by regiments: eight hussar regiments had ten companies and four of them (two further regiments had been raised) as many as twenty companies each.

During the eighteenth century Russian artillery developed rapidly. By 1757 an artillery regiment had two battalions, each of a company of bombardiers, manning howitzers and mortars, and four companies of cannoniers manning guns. Each regiment had over ninety artillery pieces of various types. In addition to the field army artillery there were numerous regiments and parks of specialized artillery of siege-guns and howitzers. Presumably because the gunners were the principal users, the pontoon regiments formed part of the artillery and not of the en-

gineers. Regimental artillery, permanently allocated to infantry or cavalry regiments, had also been increased.

The first regiment of engineers, an offshoot of the artillery, was formed in 1728 of two companies of miners, two of sappers, and two construction companies.

Catherine the Great

During the Seven Years War (1756–63) Russian troops took the field against Frederick the Great's Prussia. They enjoyed alternating fortunes, and distinguished themselves by their tenacity. It appeared that Frederick must be finally defeated, when suddenly the Russian Empress Elisabeth died. Her unstable successor, Peter III, an admirer of the King of Prussia, hastened to make peace, but within six months he had been deposed by his own German wife who subsequently became Catherine II, or Catherine the Great.

Catherine reigned from 1762 to 1796 and was

Non-commissioned officer clerk and a private of a dragoon regiment, c. 1800

regiments were raised, mainly from the Ukrainian mounted militia, bringing the infantry strength of the field army to sixty-two regiments of 132 battalions, totalling 111,000 men; but she reverted to the old organization of two battalions to a regiment, each of six companies. The fusilier battalions were renamed musketeers (although this was only a temporary redesignation) and each had a grenadier company. The eighty-four battalions of garrison infantry, mostly of six companies, were given operational tasks, sixty-five of them being allocated to frontier defence.

The cavalry, too, was reorganized once more and in 1763 Catherine introduced carabineers – cavalrymen armed with carbine and sword, but differing from dragoons in that they carried no bayonet. These were raised by converting five dragoon and six horse grenadier regiments. To replace the dragoon regiments thus lost, further units were raised, mainly from the Ukraine, bringing the total number of dragoon regiments up to twenty-three. The five ancient 'town Cossack' regiments, sometimes known as the Cherkassy or Dnieper Cossacks, and the twelve existing regiments of hussars, were converted to eleven new hussar regiments and four lancer regiments. The three cavalry regiments, privately maintained by the *Hetman* of the Ukraine Cossacks, were taken over by the St Petersburg Government. In the newly-reformed regiments the heavy cavalry and dragoons each had five squadrons, while the light cavalry (hussars and uhlan lancers) had six. Each squadron could be broken down into half-squadrons (companies). After the reorganization there were in all, sixty regular cavalry regiments of 315 squadrons, totalling 50,000 men which did not, of course, include the Cossack *sotni* or the Ukrainian mounted militia.

Under Catherine the artillery was expanded to five regiments, one of bombardiers, two of cannoniers, and two of fusiliers. Each artillery regiment had two battalions, each of five companies. The pontoniers, still only a company strong, remained as part of the artillery. In 1793, at the time of the French Revolutionary War, a further seven battalions of bombardiers were raised, but not until 1794 was the first company of horse artillery brought into existence.

Empress of all the Russias at the time of the French Revolution, and the Revolutionary and Napoleonic Wars. Catherine claimed to be an enlightened patron of the arts and sciences, as indeed she was, and a social reformer, which, all things considered, she was not. Her interests were Russian and were centred on the aggrandizement of Imperial Russia by political or military means, and she took a close interest in the strength and organization of the Russian Army.

At the time of Catherine's accession the line infantry in the field army consisted of fifty-three regiments of 160 battalions, 80,000 men in all. Garrison infantry comprised forty-seven regiments of ninety-nine battalions, totalling 65,000 men. The cavalry had fifty-two regiments of 265 squadrons, amounting to 40,000 men, and thirty-eight regiments of regular or territorial Ukrainian Cossacks outside the so-called 'irregular' troops of the main Don, Terek, and Siberian Hosts. Together the regular infantry and cavalry made up 320,000 men.

In the first two years of her reign Catherine completely reformed her army. New infantry

Throughout Catherine's long reign, the numerical strength of the Russian Army grew slowly but steadily, particularly in the cavalry arm. The guard cavalry regiments remained at five squadrons, but, after 1775, all cavalry was increased to six squadrons except for the dragoons, which were raised to ten, and the Cossack regiments which had eight *sotni*.

By 1790 the standing Russian Army had a strength of half a million men.[1]

Russia makes War in Europe

From the death of Peter the Great in 1725 until the accession of Catherine the Great in 1762, Russia lacked strong government. Most of the monarchs were women and the succession was usually disputed by force, the decision being determined by the officers of the palace guards. Ultimate power rested in the guards regiments in St Petersburg.

Yet in spite of its internal weaknesses Imperial Russia remained a power to be reckoned with in central and eastern Europe. This it owed to the strength of its standing army.

From 1726 to the end of the Seven Years War in 1763 Russia remained allied to Austria, the alliance being based on a mutual hostility towards the Ottoman Empire and a joint interest in dominating Poland. Russia again defeated the Swedes in 1743 and was ceded part of Karelia. The situation in Central Europe was changing, however, with the rising power of Prussia, whose monarch, Frederick the Great, with the backing of the French, had recently overrun Austrian Silesia. Maria Theresa, the Austrian Empress, was determined to recover the lost provinces and she entered into agreements with London and St Petersburg preparatory to a new war. Meanwhile Frederick the Great, by his personal unpopularity, had lost much of his support in Versailles. Prussia's position had deteriorated even further in that Britain, fearing Frederick's designs on Hanover, signed a treaty in 1755 with the Empress Elisabeth, by the terms of which, in

The standard of an infantry grenadier regiment of household troops with shaft crest and tassel, *c.* 1800

exchange for British gold, a force of 55,000 Russian troops were to be concentrated on the East Prussian frontier. Hanover was, therefore, to be protected from the Baltic.

In 1756 Frederick the Great made a pre-emptive attack on Saxony because he believed that failure to do so would result in a joint offensive being launched on him by Austrian, Russian, Saxon, and possibly French troops. The odds against Frederick were immense. In 1756 he had defeated the Saxons but the next year he failed against the Austrians, and the Russians invaded East Prussia. In 1758 Britain, motivated by opposition to France, changed sides; but Prussia had no other ally. In August of that same year, however, the Prussians defeated the Russians at Zorndorf in the bloodiest battle of the war, but this costly victory was of little comfort since that October Frederick lost once more to the Austrians at Hochkirch in Saxony, and in the following year, in 1759, was decisively defeated by the Russian commander, Saltykov. By 1760 Berlin was occupied once again. Yet Prussia still continued in the war, when a little more energy on

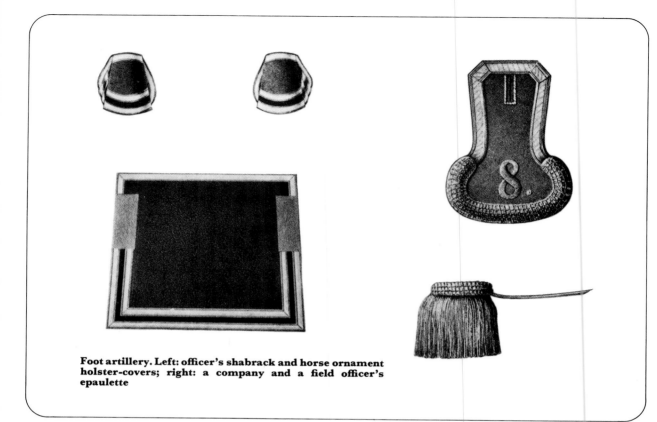

Foot artillery. Left: officer's shabrack and horse ornament holster-covers; right: a company and a field officer's epaulette

the part of the Russians, should have destroyed it.

The death of the Empress Elisabeth at the end of 1761 saved Prussia. Her loss was keenly felt in the Russian Army, for Elisabeth had interested herself in military matters and had gained much popularity by restoring to Russia much of its self-confidence and national pride.

The new Emperor, Peter III, born Karl Peter Ulrich of Holstein, was a German admirer of Prussia. He ordered the immediate withdrawal of all Russian troops from Germany, asking for nothing in return, since he was interested merely in his native Holstein's quarrel with Denmark. To wage war against Denmark he needed Frederick's neutrality. Within six months Peter was dead, probably murdered by officers of the guard with the connivance of his wife, who had herself crowned Catherine II.

Catherine, although a German, was not pro-Prussian. She made a peace with Frederick on grounds of expediency, which cost her, however, the friendship of France and Austria. But Catherine's immediate interest was the elimination of Poland. The first partition in 1772 took Russian frontiers westwards to the Dvina and upper Dnieper; the second, in 1793, took in most of Belorussia, Volhynia, and Podolia; while the third, in 1795, took Russia to the Niemen and the Bug and absorbed Lithuania and Podlesia into the Empire. Poland disappeared, divided up between Russia, Prussia, and Austria, and was not to re-emerge as a national state, except for a brief Napoleonic interlude, until 1918.

Peter the Great had been largely unsuccessful in his wars against the Turks, but in 1738, after the Third Treaty of Vienna, Russia and Austria had attempted to encroach once more on Turkish territory. The Empress Anne's Russian troops invaded the Turkish North Black Sea littoral and the Crimea. The Turko-Tartar resistance was fierce, however, and Anne gained nothing except the cession of the port of Azov, giving to Russia the control of the estuary of the Don.

Catherine was moved both by Russian interests and by personal ambition and vainglory. She wanted to eliminate Turkey in the Black Sea area and in the Balkans and even dreamed of herself as head of the Orthodox Greek Church in an

Grenadier head-dress 1811–16. Left: a non-commissioned officer; right: two grenadiers

Islam-free Constantinople. The Turks, on the other hand, made anxious by the Russian threat to dominate and eventually liquidate Poland, and incited by French diplomacy, decided to strike before Russia should become too powerful. War was declared in 1768. Turkey, however, was the loser, for Russian troops speedily overran Moldavia and Wallachia and the Crimea, while Russian men-of-war, partly officered and manned by the British Navy, sailed from the Baltic to the Black Sea and destroyed a Turkish fleet off the coast of Asia Minor. By the Treaty of Kuchuk Kainarji in 1774, Russia returned to Turkey her conquests of Georgia, Moldavia, Wallachia, and Bessarabia, but was given the control of the Kerch Straits and access into the Black Sea.

These gains, however, merely whetted the appetite of Imperial Russia. Catherine, an adventuress and opportunist, annexed the Crimea in 1784 and, on the death of Maria Theresa, hastened to come to an alliance with Joseph II of Austria. The Turkish Sultan, sufficiently provoked, declared war on Russia and fought a successful campaign against both Austria and

Russia. Under Potemkin, the Empress's favourite, Russian troops had little success until they stormed the great fortresses of Ochakov on the Dniester in 1788, and Izmail on the Danube in 1790. The credit for these successes belonged to Suvorov, the outstanding general of tsarist Russia.

The Influence of Suvorov

Alexander Vasilevich Suvorov has become such a legend both in tsarist and in communist Russia, that it is difficult to establish the limitation of his talents. Born in 1730 he was, according to the popular account, a puny and sickly child. He appears to have had some education, for he could write in French, German, and Polish tolerably well, and he was a great reader. He was supposed to have entered the army as a private soldier at the age of fifteen, but was not commissioned as an officer until nine years later, in April 1754. It is possible that this was in fact the case; on the other

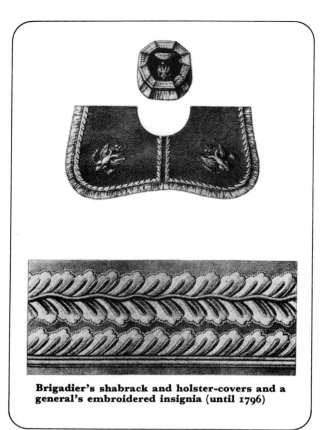

Brigadier's shabrack and holster-covers and a general's embroidered insignia (until 1796)

great stamina, coupled with an indolent nature and a lack of individuality and initiative. Suvorov was able to exploit the soldier's strength and to minimize the effect of his weaknesses.

Training was reduced to that level which could be understood by the illiterate of the meanest intelligence and was reinforced by a host of easily remembered maxims. This well suited the Russian mentality. The most widely known of these – 'the bullet is a fool, the bayonet is a fine fellow (*molodets*)' – might be regarded as unsound doctrine, but in fact it was based on the conditions of the time. The Russian infantryman's musket was slow to load and inaccurate when fired. The praise of the bayonet made him more ready to close with the enemy, and he fought best in close column under the eyes of his officers. In some respects Suvorov was ahead of his time in that all training had to have a purpose. The relationship between himself and his commanders, and in particular between commanders and troops, were easier and less formal than the harsh unthinking methods used elsewhere in central Europe. And he himself understood the value to the troops' morale of the direct personal appeal.

Suvorov was the author of two well-known books, *The Science of Victory* and *The Seven Laws of War*.

Although Suvorov is considered in Russia to be one of the world's greatest generals, it is doubtful whether he was among the foremost captains. Suvorov's strength lay in his sense of realism and his ability to reduce the art of war to its essentials. He was a tactician and not a strategist and the basis of his tactics was that boldness always pays; his only formula was that of moving quickly to the attack. Flexibility was entirely lacking. Suvorov's methods did much to improve the fighting efficiency and the morale of the infantry; on the other hand, in typical Russian fashion, losses meant nothing to him, for he would rather waste lives than powder. In front of the walls of Izmail his order contained the words, 'to seize the fortress by assault, *without regard to losses*'. By nature he was entirely brutal.

Suvorov led the Russian troops against Poland and took Warsaw in October 1794, for which Catherine the Great had him promoted to field-marshal. Two years later, when Paul came to the

hand it is not unlikely that his *name* was entered on the lists of the regiment when he was fifteen, but that he himself did not join until a later date, and then as a *Fanenjunker* or other-rank officer aspirant. Aspiring guards officers were sometimes entered on the rolls of their regiments when they were still in the cradle.

During the Seven Years War, Suvorov fought with distinction and was present when the victorious Russian troops entered Berlin in October 1760. By the end of the war, still in his early thirties, he commanded a regiment and he soon won renown for his insistence on realistic battle training, for he was an outstanding leader of men.

Suvorov's success lay in his understanding of the characteristics and simple capabilities of Russian infantry. Two centuries of the Tartar yoke, serfdom, the absolute despotism of the Tsars, the severity of the climate, and the harshness of living conditions, had bred into the soldier passive obstinacy, unthinking obedience, and an exaggerated respect for rank. The Russian soldier – and this applied, too, to his officer – had courage and throne, Suvorov was retired and exiled to the country. For the Emperor Paul had strong opinions on military matters and they were much at variance with those of Suvorov.

The Gatchina Corps

Paul was Catherine the Great's eldest son and his father was assumed to be Tsar Peter III, the monarch who, after only six months' reign, was murdered with the complicity of his own wife. Paul had no sympathy and little affection for his mother, while she had little regard for his talents, being jealous and fearful in case he should replace her. Because of the peculiarity of the precedents and the law relating to the imperial succession, the monarch at that time exercised the right to nominate his or her successor. Paul suspected, not without reason, that his mother Catherine intended to disinherit him and nominate as her successor Paul's eldest son (her own grandson) Alexander Pavlevich. This preyed on his mind and, resentful at his exclusion from the councils of state, caused him to withdraw entirely from the Imperial Court at the Winter Palace in St Petersburg.

Paul moved with his wife and immediate entourage (but not with his two eldest sons who remained in the care of Catherine) to Gatchina, a town about fifty miles south-west of St Petersburg. There he remained until the forty-second year of his life. He was a curious man of a somewhat unstable temperament who could by turns be suspicious, vindictive, cruel, liberal, and generous. He had great sympathy for the Poles and made no secret of his opposition to the war being waged against them by his mother. He regarded the French as oppressors of Europe and disapproved of his mother's reluctance to enter the Allied coalitions against the revolutionaries. Paul was in the main pro-German and he expressed the greatest of admiration for the Prussians. This gave rise to further contradictions, for like his father and his great-grandfather he dearly loved to play the soldier and he ran his household, his suite, and the Gatchina Court, on Prussian military lines. All activities were regulated by the

An officer of the Hussar Life Guards, *c.* 1798

drum-beat. A corps of troops was stationed there under his command and he was permitted to parade and drill this corps at his pleasure. By his direction, the training methods and the uniform of the troops there were altered to conform to the Prussian pattern. The Tsarevich became largely absorbed in the minutiae of military rules and dress regulations, an interest which he passed on to both of his sons, Alexander and Nicholas.

The military methods of this little Potsdam of the north were extremely harsh, even allowing for the conditions of the time. The Gatchina Colonel of Artillery was Arakcheev, a man who was later to be responsible for the pattern of Russian military development for nearly a quarter of a century.

The Emperor Paul

The Empress Catherine the Great died suddenly without dictating her wishes as to the succession.

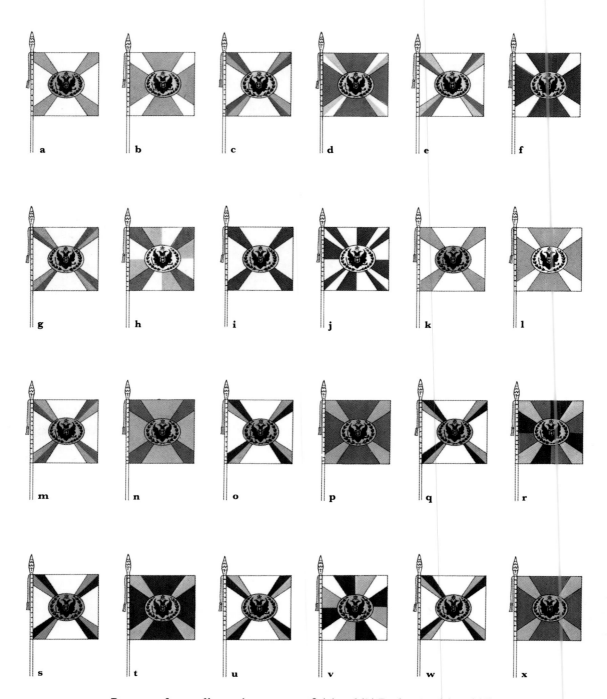

Banners of grenadier regiments, *c*. 1798. (a) and (b) Pavlovsky, (c) and (d) Ekaterinoslavsky, (e) and (f) Little Russian, (g) and (h) Sibirsky, (i) and (j) St Petersburg, (k) and (l) Astrakhansky, (m) and (n) Fanogorisky, (o) and (p) Khersonsky, (q) and (r) Kievsky, (s) and (t) Moskovsky, (u) and (v) Tavrichesky, (w) and (x) Caucasian

And so Paul came to the throne. The Gatchina battalions, in their obsolete and cumbersome Prussian-type uniforms, moved into the Winter Palace.

Paul had long feared that instead of becoming Tsar he would be imprisoned or murdered by Catherine's successor. His suspicions were not entirely baseless for there had been at least two such murders in recent memory. Peter III and Ivan VI had both been done to death at the instigation of Paul's own mother. Nor were his worries lighter when he came to the throne for he continued to fear a usurper. He became increasingly eccentric and his form of government was based on a never-ending series of personal *ukazy*, many liberal but most of them repressive. Although hardly the champion of the serfs, he attempted to restrict many of the abuses against them, and this displeased the landowning nobility. He made no secret of his dislike of the regiments of the guard, and gave preference to officers of the Gatchina corps. He enforced the Gatchina methods and style of uniform on the rest of the army. Many of his actions were rational and some of them were just, but he alienated too many factions and he failed to make good his threat, in the interest of his own safety, to exile the imperial guard regiments to the distant outposts of the Empire. He was subject, too, to great rages which made his family and suite fear him.

Russia's foreign policy under Paul, although not irrational, became increasingly incoherent. Napoleon had, on his way to Egypt, seized Malta from the Grand Master of the Order of St John. This incensed Paul and in 1798 he accepted, from the Volhynian Priory of the Maltese Order, the Grand Mastership, introducing the new titles and badges of the Order into the guards cavalry corps. Great Britain succeeded in persuading Paul to enter the Second Coalition arrayed against the French. Paul gave a stately home and generous pension to Louis XVIII, the exiled Bourbon King of France, against the time when he should be returned to his rightful throne, and since Paul disapproved of Prussian reluctance to join the coalition, he broke off diplomatic relations with Berlin and concentrated an army under Kamensky against the Prussian border. In 1799 he recalled Suvorov from retirement and sent Russian troops

Ornate bridle and curb piece used by a cavalry officer of the guard; a cuirass and a cavalry overtunic, 1797–1801

to Italy to help the Austrians against the French; he gave Suvorov the new rank of *Generalissimus*, to befit his new dignity as the Allied Commander-in-Chief.

Suvorov, having crossed the Alps, took Milan and Turin and won the battles of Trebbia and Novi, preparatory to invading France. But, as he could not agree with the Austrians, he moved north into Switzerland to join a second Russian army under Korsakov. Meanwhile, however, the Italian Jew, Masséna, formerly in the ranks of the Sardinian Army but now a high-ranking general in the French revolutionary forces, defeated Korsakov near Zürich before Suvorov could join him.

This moved Paul to anger. He recalled Suvorov and made a break with Austria as the author of his misfortunes. He quarrelled with England over the British occupation of Malta and returned to the policy initiated by Catherine the Great in the earliest days of the Revolutionary War, signing with Sweden and Denmark a treaty of armed neutrality directed against Britain. The Bourbon pretender Louis XVIII was flung out of his

Left: a non-commissioned officer of the Belonissian Hussars; right: a soldier of Tatarsky and a non-commissioned officer of Litovsky (Lithuanian) Cavalry

grace-and-favour estate at Mitau. By 1801 it was impossible to tell who was regarded by Paul as his foe. Theoretically he was at war with France and he had broken off diplomatic relations with Austria. But he was ready to fight his ally England, and had sent 20,000 Cossacks eastward to invade India.

In March 1801, by a palace *coup* in which Pahlen, the Governor-General of St Petersburg, and a small group of army officers together with the Semenovsky Guards took part, Paul was murdered. He was deposed, it is believed, with the foreknowledge of his son and successor Alexander.

The Army under Alexander I

Alexander had been a constant visitor to Gatchina when his father was still a grand duke, and he and his two brothers, Constantine and Nicholas, were fascinated by the drill-ground. One of their greatest pleasures was in the shouting of military-style orders and in parades and uniforms. Like his father, Alexander became increasingly under the influence of Alexei Andreevich Arakcheev, an artillery officer who had come to the Imperial notice when at Gatchina. Arakcheev was a brutal and blunt martinet, although probably an honest man, with considerable organizing abilities. Being indifferent to the opinion of others, indeed going so far as to revel in his unpopularity, he was blamed by the army for all Alexander's deficiencies.

Alexander himself was friendly and modest, going to great lengths to avoid giving offence, and having actually contrived, when Catherine was alive, to remain on good terms with both the Empress and his father. Exuding charm and grace, he was a secretive dissimulator and an accomplished actor, somewhat weak and vacillating, forming his opinions slowly and trusting no one. Like his father, he could be both autocratic and liberal. His mind was continually troubled, possibly on account of his own part in the deposing of his father. Like many of weak will, he could be extraordinarily obstinate.

Alexander wanted peace and he arranged terms with both the British and the French. The Russian relationship was uneasy, however, with both of these powers. He flirted with Prussia which had not been at war since 1795. The European peace was broken by the kidnapping in 1804 of the Duc d'Enghien on Baden territory by French agents, and his subsequent murder. For Napoleon rejected the Russian note of protest with an insulting inquiry as to 'when Alexander proposed to bring to justice the murderers of the late Tsar'. The French crossed Prussian territory, without leave, on their way to invade Austria.

The Austrians were defeated at Ulm in October of 1805, and the Russian forces under Prince Kutuzov, a soldier of popularity and some distinction who had served under Suvorov at Izmail fifteen years before, retired into Moravia. Napoleon was already in Vienna and Alexander made the journey to Olmütz in Moravia to meet Francis I of Austria and insist that the cautious Kutuzov stop his withdrawal and bring his troops to battle. Kutuzov sulkily declined, and had the conduct of operations taken from his hands by Alexander and the Austrians.

The battle at Austerlitz began at 9.00 on a wintry December day and lasted only two hours. It was Napoleon's boast that out of thirty or more battles, Austerlitz was the easiest and most decisive of his career. The Russian troops ran away, cursing the Austrians as they did so, and both Alexander and Francis had to flee for their lives. This was Alexander's lesson that war was not to be learned on the parade-ground and that he himself was without ability as a field commander. After the battle he wept, blaming Kutuzov for not having insisted more strongly on avoiding battle.

Russian troops were not temperamentally suited to fighting alongside allies, being by nature suspicious and obstinate to the point of arrogance. An earlier Anglo-Russian expeditionary force in the Low Countries had been a failure. A second Anglo-Russian expedition made up of 5,000 British and 13,000 Russians, together with a Neapolitan army of 40,000, had more fortune in 1805 in that they cleared the French from Italy.

By then Austria was out of the war and Masséna returned to the south, overrunning the whole of the Italian mainland by the spring of 1806. The expeditionary force was evacuated.

Alexander's attention reverted once more to Prussia, with whom he concluded a secret agreement. On 26 September 1806 the King of Prussia sent an ultimatum to Napoleon demanding that French troops quit German territory east of the Rhine. Napoleon's reply was to march troops which inflicted two successive defeats of the Prussian Army at Jena and Auerstädt. On 25 October Napoleon entered Berlin and French troops occupied Prussian Poland as far east as Warsaw. Russia was now directly vulnerable to the French Army which had arrived at its frontier. On 26 December Bennigsen, a Hanoverian soldier of fortune in command of the Russian forces, repulsed a French foray near Warsaw.

Two months later Bennigsen met Napoleon again at Preussisch-Eylau in East Prussia. He claimed a further repulse, while Napoleon

Troopers of the Kurlandsky and Pereyaslavsky Dragoon Regiments, c. 1806

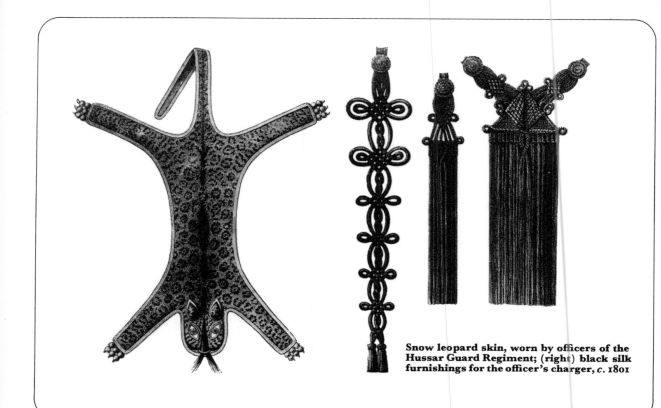

Snow leopard skin, worn by officers of the Hussar Guard Regiment; (right) black silk furnishings for the officer's charger, c. 1801

regarded the battle as a French victory. The Russians had a numerical superiority yet the engagement cost them in casualties 26,000 dead.

The Russian position had been much weakened by a new war against Turkey. Prussia had been overrun by the French, except in the north-east corner. The British subsidy to Russia was inadequate and there was a lack of mutual trust between London and St Petersburg. Alexander was particularly irritated by British reluctance (because of the Prussian seizure of Hanover) to afford any assistance to Prussia and London's refusal to land British troops in northern Europe. Meanwhile Bennigsen's 50,000 Russians gave battle at Friedland in June 1807, but they were decisively defeated by less than half their number of Frenchmen. Alexander asked Napoleon for peace.

The Treaty of Tilsit had far-reaching provisions. A new state, the Polish Grand Duchy of Warsaw, was resurrected with the King of Saxony as its head. The Polish province of Bialystok went to Russia. Prussia lost its Polish territories and all lands west of the Elbe. The rest of Europe was to be drawn into a coalition against Great Britain. In 1809 Russia, encouraged by Napoleon to do so, went to war with Sweden and occupied and annexed Swedish Finland. The war with Turkey in the Balkans dragged on until 1812. Only Austria dared to take up arms again against Napoleon.

The Long Armistice

Having asked Alexander in vain for a Romanov as his new bride, Napoleon turned to the Austrian Habsburgs. It appeared that the relations between France and Austria would henceforth be on a more friendly footing. Alexander, however, was suspicious of the Franco-Austrian accord and, fearing dissension among his Polish subjects, was sensitive to the new Polish Duchy set up by Napoleon on the Russian frontier. Russia was the main loser by the new anti-British alliance since the main importer of the Empire's goods was Britain, and the loss of customs revenue to the government contributed to the steady depreciation of the currency. At the end of 1810, in a fit of pique against the French, St Petersburg replied by the imposition of a heavy tax on the importation by land of luxury goods, which in fact were mainly of French origin. Paris protested. In December of that year and during January of 1811 Napoleon annexed to France the whole of the north German coast, including the Duchy of Oldenburg, which belonged by marriage to Alexander's sister, Catherine.

During 1811 the uneasy truce with Napoleon became more strained and Alexander looked about for allies. The Austrian royal house, linked by marriage with France, was for the moment disinterested. Prussia was too fearful. Russia did, however, improve its relations with Sweden. Meanwhile Kutuzov, in command in the south, was ordered to come to terms with the Turks. By the Treaty of Bucharest, Alexander abandoned the Serbs to their fate and gave up his conquests of Wallachia and Moldavia, keeping only Bessarabia, the eastern portion of Moldavia between the Dniester and the Pruth. Alexander then looked to Britain for another alliance.

Alexander had made use of the remaining two years of peace to improve the efficiency of his armed forces. In 1810 Arakcheev left the War Ministry to undertake the reorganization of the artillery and the supply of all warlike equipment. His successor as War Minister was a Livonian, Barclay de Tolly.

There had been some change in the field grouping, in accordance with the Napoleonic pattern, the tactical formation now being the division. The infantry of the field army was, by 1812, made up of 170 regiments of 511 battalions, there being three battalions to the regiment.[2] On mobilization, however, this number of active field battalions was due to be reduced to 401, since the second battalion in each regiment was to find reinforcements to bring the first and third battalions to full strength and throw off an élite company, these companies being grouped into new grenadier battalions. The remnant of the second battalion became the depot battalion for the mobilized regiment of two field battalions. A guard battalion at war strength numbered 764 men, and one of the line 732.

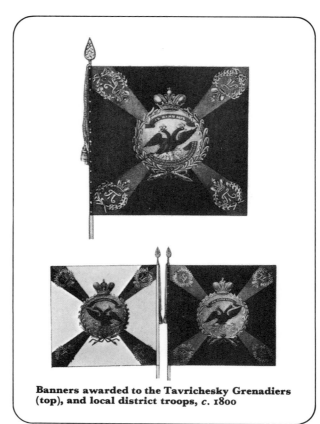

Banners awarded to the Tavrichesky Grenadiers (top), and local district troops, c. 1800

The 170 first-line infantry regiments were formed into twenty-eight divisions (six regiments to the division of which two were light infantry). Of these twenty-eight divisions, eighteen were deployed in the west, four in Moldavia, three in Finland, two in the Caucasus, and one on the Black Sea.

In addition to the 284,000 first-line infantry of the field force there were 103 garrison infantry battalions and 216 infantry battalions of the reserve, in all another 230,000 men, organised into eighteen reserve divisions, numbered from 30 to 47 inclusive. These divisions had a command and administrative, rather than a tactical, function; for the battalions were drafted into the field army after the war started, and the reserve divisions eventually disbanded.

In 1811 there were seventy regiments of regular cavalry, totalling 440 squadrons, of which eighty-one squadrons formed the depot squadrons in time of war.[3] The remaining 359 field formation squadrons numbered 49,000 horse. These troops, including the guard and Ukrainian Cossacks, were regular cavalry. The Emperor could easily raise,

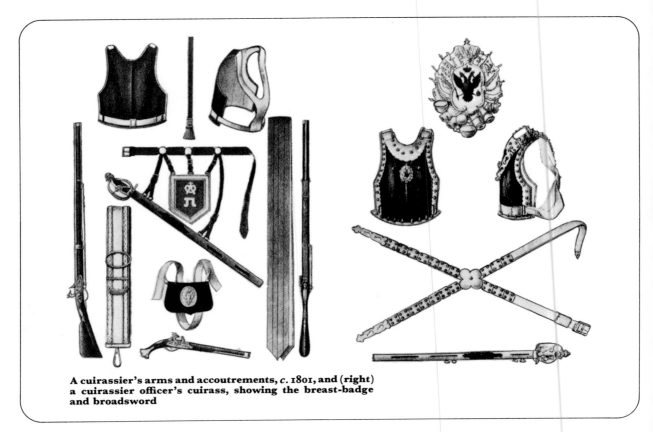

A cuirassier's arms and accoutrements, *c.* 1801, and (right) a cuirassier officer's cuirass, showing the breast-badge and broadsword

however, a further 100,000 cavalry from the Cossack hosts, at least eighty-two regiments from the Don, ten from the Black Sea, fifteen from the Ukraine, and more elsewhere. It was to these so-called 'cavalry irregulars', particularly to the Cossacks of the Don, that Kutuzov owed much of his success during the French retreat in 1812 and 1813.

There were twelve regular cavalry regiments in Moldavia, two in Finland, and three in the Caucasus. The remaining fifty-three were in the west.

The artillery totalled 159 batteries/companies of which thirty-two were depot companies.[4] Each company of foot artillery was 250 men strong and was equipped with twelve guns. Horse artillery batteries usually varied by designation. Heavy batteries had four twenty-pounders and eight twelve-pounders, while light batteries had four twelve-pounders and eight six-pounders. Divisional artillery brigades normally had one heavy and one light company.

The engineer corps comprised twenty-four companies of pioneers and the same number of pontoon companies which, by 1812, had been taken over from the artillery.

In all the Russian Army in 1812 numbered 700,000 men not including the Cossack hosts or the *opolchenie*, the home guard militia.

In the early summer of 1812 the troops in western Russia were deployed in three armies. The first, under Barclay de Tolly (who still retained his post as Minister of War), of six infantry corps and four of cavalry, was made up of 127,000 men and 500 guns. The second, under Bagration, of two infantry corps and two of cavalry, had only 45,000 men and 200 guns, while the third, under Tormazov, of three small corps and a corps of cavalry, totalled 46,000 men and 160 guns.[5]

The War of 1812

The last approach to reason was made by the Tsar to the French Ambassador, General Lauriston, in April of that year. Alexander said that he was prepared to accept the indemnity offered by France to the Duke of Oldenburg and would modify the Russian customs system which discriminated against French imports. On the other hand, he insisted on freedom to trade with neutrals as he thought fit and, fearful for his own security, demanded that French troops should evacuate Swedish Pomerania and Prussia. He went so far as to say that if there was any reinforcement of the French garrisons on the Vistula he would consider this to be an act of war.

Napoleon made no reply to these demands but kept up diplomatic activity merely to gain time, for he had already decided to invade Russia. In May the French Emperor arrived in Dresden preparatory to taking over the field command. Alexander was already at Vilna with his armies.

Against the Russian covering forces of about 225,000, Napoleon's Grand Army numbered over 500,000, but only a half were Frenchmen. The remainder of the force were Germans, Poles, Italians, Spaniards, Portuguese, and Croats, many of them doubtful and unwilling allies. On 24 June 1812, without a formal declaration of war, the Grand Army crossed the Niemen on its way into Russia.

Alexander's presence at the field headquarters was an embarrassment to the Russian High Command. No Russian Commander-in-Chief had been appointed. Kutuzov was still in the south and Alexander had heartily disliked him from the day of Austerlitz. In default, the mantle fell on Barclay de Tolly, the War Minister who, at this time, was also the commander of 1 Army, by far the largest in the field. But, as the Emperor's minister, he had to refer all his orders to Alexander.

Alexander lacked a practical mind, and was later to become obsessed with mysticism. He was continually seeking a new revolutionary approach to warfare and a solution of the military problems of the day. These were provided by Pfuel, a Prussian colonel in the Russian service who, much to the irritation of Barclay de Tolly's staff, advocated a huge defensive bastion to be set up on the banks of the Drissa. Alexander had been so impressed with the proposal that thousands of workmen had been employed excavating earthworks. The ideas and the defences had no bearing on the war. Arakcheev, Balashev, and Shishkov

Non-commissioned officer and privates of 24, 25, and 26 Eger Regiments, in walking out, undress, and parade uniform, c. 1807

petitioned the Tsar that he should leave the army and return to his capital for, they rightly argued, the supreme command should be given only to a subject whom the sovereign would be free to dismiss, should it be necessary. Otherwise the monarch would bear the responsibility, in the eyes of his peoples, for defeats which none could avoid. Remembering Austerlitz, Alexander left, firstly for Moscow and then for St Petersburg.

Barclay sent Wittgenstein's corps towards the Baltic to cover the Dvina and approaches to the capital, and Napoleon followed suit by detaching 70,000 men to the north under Macdonald and Oudinot. These troops formed what was in effect another theatre. An Austrian corps faced Tormazov in Volhynia. Yet further to the south Admiral Chichagov with 35,000 men was still in Moravia. The main campaign was to be fought in western and central Russia, to the north of the Pripet Marshes.

As Barclay showed no inclination to stand and fight, but retired steadily eastwards, Napoleon tried to cut off Bagration and prevent his rejoining Barclay by thrusting Davout's 1 French Corps

Trumpeter of the Mariupol Hussar Regiment, *c.* **1801**

between the two armies. It seems likely that Bagration would have been destroyed if Jerome Bonaparte, Napoleon's brother, had acted with more dispatch. As it was, Bagration escaped by marching steadily to the south-east, and after a circuitous passage he joined Barclay in Smolensk at the beginning of August.

Early in July, when Bagration believed himself to be isolated and surrounded, he wrote to Arakcheev urging in the bluntest terms that Barclay should attack in the centre and not rely on the defences of 'Mr Pfuel', for these, said Bagration, would surely be outflanked. Condemning the Russians for retreating like Prussians (the Prussians were held in little regard as soldiers at this time), Bagration used strong language, judging, but not naming, the man who ordered the withdrawal as a traitor to the Tsar and the country. Bagration had little idea of the enemy strength facing the Russians; he himself believed it insignificant. In fact there can be no doubt that Barclay, and Kutuzov after him, were right in withdrawing. But the discontent that Bagration voiced was widespread, and made the corps commander Constantine, Alexander's brother, ask whether Barclay, intent on sacrificing the whole Empire, was bound for the White Sea.

In the second week in August Napoleon arrived at Smolensk where Barclay was drawn up awaiting him. By then the strength of the French force had shrunk to about 200,000 men, thinned by the corps detached to the north and south, by the many stragglers and deserters, particularly among the non-French element, and by heat and sickness casualties. Some fighting had taken place on the distant northern and southern flanks, with results by no means unfavourable to the Russians, for Wittgenstein gave a good account of himself at the battle of Polotsk while Tormazov pinned down the Austrian corps as well as Reynier's French corps sent to extricate it. Against his inclination and judgement Barclay decided to give battle.

Shortly before the Battle of Smolensk was fought, General Sir Robert Wilson, with the British Military Commission serving in Russia, arrived at the scene of operations, and he has left some revealing descriptions of his impressions of the Russian soldier at this time. Wilson might be judged to be a Russophil, for he could hardly have

Cannonier and company officer of foot artillery, 1808

A miner and a *pionier* from 1 Pionier Regiment, c. 1806

survived in this appointment if he were not. Some of his comment probably has an underlying propaganda theme in that it was meant to endear the Russian ally to a British public, which in the past was none too sure whether the Russian was friend or foe.

Wilson describes the Russian infantrymen as 'between the ages of eighteen and forty, short, stocky and strong, inured to weather and hardships and the scantiest of food, accustomed to laborious toils and the carriage of heavy burthens; ferocious but disciplined; obstinately brave, patient, docile and obedient; devoted to their sovereign, their chief and their country'. All of this was undoubtedly true.

'The Russian soldier, continues Wilson, is extremely subordinate and attached to his officer, who treats him with a peculiar kindness and not as a machine, but as a reasonable being. Punishment is not so frequent as in other armies, nor is it so very severe. The Russian officer, although frequently making the greatest physical exertion, is, however, inclined to indolent habits when not on duty, he loves his sleep after food and dislikes to walk or ride far. No troops can and do defend so well in retreat.'

Another Englishman, Robert Porter, was much intrigued by what he saw of the free Cossacks of the Don Host, in which each trooper furnished at his own expense horse, uniform, and arms. Of them Porter says:

'Their persons, air, and appointments and the animals on which they are mounted, seem so totally at variance, that you can hardly suppose a reason for so unequal a union. The men are robust and fit for service; their horses appear completely the reverse; mean in shape and slouching in motion, every limb speaks of languor and every moment you expect to see them drop down dead under their heavy burthen; but so false are these shows, that there is not a more hardy animal existing; it will travel incalculable journeys and remain exposed to the heat or cold, day and night, without manifesting any sense of inconvenience. They never know the luxury of a snug stable and a well littered bed, nor ever enjoy the comfort of a currycomb or a wisp of straw. Their sustenance is of the most scanty sort.'

From Smolensk to Borodino

Since Barclay was insistent that he should first secure his withdrawal route to Moscow before accepting battle, he dispatched Bagration's 2 Army to Dorogobuzh, about eight miles further east. Raevsky's 7 Corps inside Smolensk was relieved by Dokhturov's 6 Corps.

On the afternoon of 17 August Napoleon directed Ney, Davout, and Poniatowsky against the defences in front of the suburbs and before evening had reached the city walls. By nightfall much of Smolensk was on fire and Russian losses had been heavy – estimated at 20,000. Barclay de Tolly gave the order for the retreat to be resumed and by daybreak the Russian columns were already several miles to the east. The next day, on the Valutina plateau due east of Smolensk, Barclay was attacked again by Ney. If Junot had co-operated in the outflanking movement Barclay would have lost a large part of his remaining 100,000 men.

Barclay de Tolly was in a precarious personal position *vis-à-vis* both Russian generals and troops. Although nominally in command, he was junior to Bagration. The Russian is chauvinistic and too ready to cry treason, and no one is more suspicious of strangers and foreigners. As a Livonian, Barclay was regarded as a foreigner, for it is said that he was more fluent in German than in Russian. There were of course a great number of Livonian and German officers in the service of the Tsar, some of them corps commanders, so that Bagration, Barclay's most outspoken critic, who bore the non-Russian title of the royal house of Georgia, complained that 'there were so many Germans that a Russian could not breathe'. And so on 29 August Prince Kutuzov, a man of great popularity in the Russian Army, arrived to take over the post of Commander-in-Chief in the West. His arrival restored, albeit temporarily, the morale of the tired and dispirited troops. Barclay returned to the command of 1 Army.

Kutusov, who was both cautious and strong-

Kettle-drummers from the Sibirsky, Orenburgsky, and Ingermanlandsky Dragoon Regiments, *c*. 1801

willed, had in his time been a commander of distinction. His name was linked with Suvorov, dead twelve years before, and he had seen long service against the French and the Turks. But now he was a few years short of his seventieth birthday, sick and prematurely old. Too gross to sit a horse, he travelled everywhere by carriage, and his indifferent health caused him to sleep eighteen hours a day.

Napoleon, too, had lost much of his fire and, as an Emperor, had lost touch with some of the realities of war. His main error, however, lay in his lack of a political aim, for in invading Russia he had intended no more than teaching Alexander a sharp military lesson that the man of destiny could not be defied. He had hoped to do this in one short campaign, possibly in one or two pitched battles. Napoleon believed, in company with many European statesmen that as soon as the Grand Army had made a deep penetration into Russia, Alexander would submit, particularly if Moscow appeared to be threatened. But, in fact, the French Emperor had not been able to bring the elusive Barclay to battle, except for the un-

Ryadovoi, Guards Cavalry Corps, everyday uniform, 1799–1800

A

1 Fusilier, Kievsky Grenadier Regiment, winter field service uniform, 1797–1801
2 Nestroevoi Serzhant, Infantry Regiment, walking-out dress, 1786–96
3 St Petersburg Grenadier, winter general service uniform, 1808

B

MICHAEL YOUENS

1 Officer of Horse Artillery, summer
  general service uniform, 1797–1801
2 Infantry General, summer parade uniform,
  1808–10
3 Unter-Ofitser, Sumsky Hussars, summer
  parade dress, 1797–1801

1

2

3

1 **Bombardir, Foot Artillery, summer field service uniform, 1808–9**

2 **Unter-Ofitser, 8 Eger Regiment, winter parade uniform, 1802**

3 **Ryadovoi of Uhlans, Tsarevich Konstantin Pavlovich's Regiment, undress uniform, 1803–6**

D

Litavrshchik, Glukhovsky Cuirassiers, ceremonial parade uniform, 1802–3

E

1 **Konduktor, Engineer Corps, everyday uniform, 1812–16**

2 **Trooper, Tartar Horse Regiment, winter field service uniform, 1803–6**

3 **Unter-Ofitser, Balaclava Greek Infantry Battalion, ceremonial dress, 1797–1830**

F

1 **Unter-Ofitser, 24 Eger Regiment, walking-out dress, 1806–7**
2 **Ober-Ofitser, Kirnburnsky Dragoons, winter parade uniform, 1812–14**
3 **Ryadovoi, Liflyandsky (Livonian Horse-Eger Regiment, winter parade uniform, 1813–14**

1

2

3

MICHAEL YOUENS

G

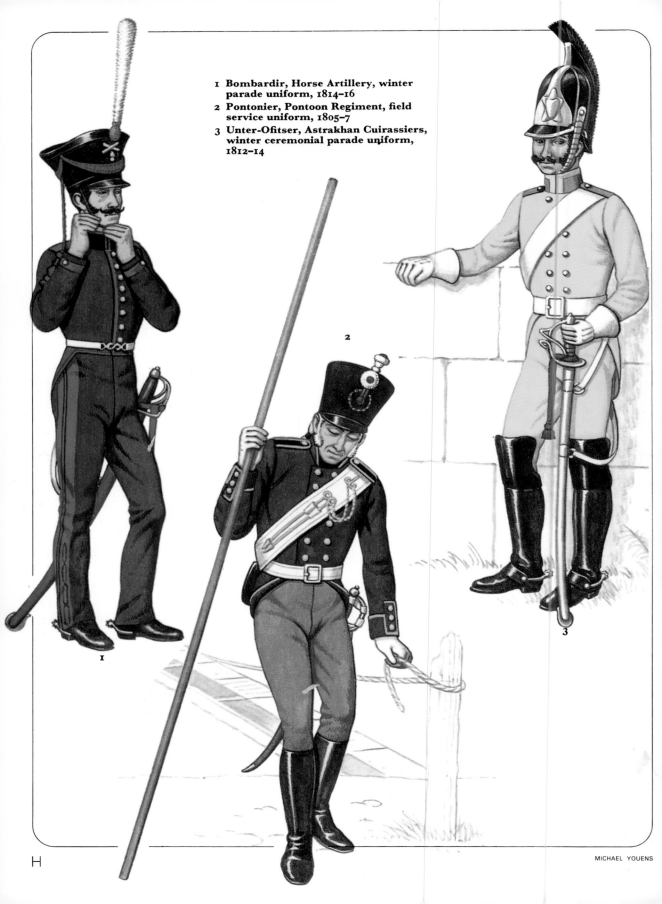

1 **Bombardir, Horse Artillery, winter parade uniform, 1814–16**
2 **Pontonier, Pontoon Regiment, field service uniform, 1805–7**
3 **Unter-Ofitser, Astrakhan Cuirassiers, winter ceremonial parade uniform, 1812–14**

H

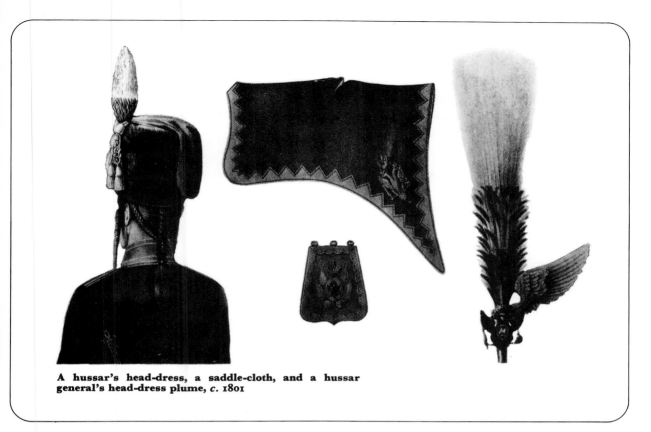

A hussar's head-dress, a saddle-cloth, and a hussar general's head-dress plume, *c.* 1801

satisfactory engagement at Smolensk, and he had wasted precious weeks awaiting in vain the peace-*parlementaires* from St Petersburg. Not until 24 August, very late in the Russian campaigning season, did he decide at last to make for Moscow.

Kutuzov had received some 30,000 reinforcements, many from the *opolchenie* of very indifferent quality, and he decided to give battle near Borodino on the main highway to Moscow. The French forces had dwindled to about 125,000 and by now were slightly outnumbered by the Russians. After a preliminary engagement on 5 September, the main battle began two days later and lasted throughout daylight. The French were left in possession of the field but their losses amounted to 30,000. Before the end of that day General Rapp, already wounded, commented to the Emperor that he 'would be forced to send in the guard'. To which Napoleon replied that he would 'take good care not to' as he did not want it destroyed. By not committing the guard Napoleon may have permitted Kutuzov to escape. But in the event, the decision was of relatively little importance, for Napoleon himself sealed the fate of the

Grand Army by remaining too long in Moscow. The weather did the rest, not Kutuzov.

Of Borodino Murat said to Ney, on the morning after the battle, that he had 'never seen anything like it for artillery fire, the armies being so close together that most of it was grape'. And, commenting yet more soberly, added 'but the Russians retired in good order'.

On 13 September Kutuzov held the celebrated council of war at Fili and decided to give up Moscow rather than destroy his army. He left the old capital, moving off south-eastwards on the Ryazan road. French troops entered the city the next day.

Moscow

Alexander had decreed for the raising of a new militia for the defence of St Petersburg and Moscow and for the creation of a new reserve in depth based on Nizhnii Novgorod. The three districts raised, respectively, 25,000, 125,000, and

Non-commissioned officer and trooper from the Litovsky-Tatarsky (Lithuanian-Tartar) Regiment of Horse, in winter uniform, *c.* **1801**

40,000 men. By far the majority of the recruits were serfs, and these took up arms either willingly or without complaint.

The Governor-General of Moscow, Count Rostopchin, had been responsible for raising the greater part of this militia from provinces as far afield as Moscow, Smolensk, Tver, Tula, Yaroslavl Vladimir, Ryazan, and Kaluga, and in an effort to sustain the morale of his new levies had depicted Kutuzov's battles as victories. As the enemy approached Moscow he assured the soldier peasantry that the city would be defended and not given up. Rostopchin never forgave Kutuzov for his decision to abandon the city.

The day after the occupation of Moscow numbers of fires broke out. Fanned by a strong north wind, they spread rapidly and gutted whole districts. French troops brought them under control; but two days later the fires flared up again. At first the Russians blamed the French for wanton destruction. Yet the evidence, such as it is, is more inclined to the view that the fires were deliberately started by Russian incendiaries. The French certainly had little motive for destroy-

ing the city, since they required the supplies and shelter which only Moscow could give. The Russians, and particularly the Cossacks, on the other hand, traditionally burned or destroyed anything which might be of use to the enemy. According to contemporary French reports most of the Russian fire-fighting equipment had already been removed and among the few arsonists taken in the act were Russian police officials.

The fire has never been satisfactorily explained, but the likelihood is that it was Russian work, whether instigated by Rostopchin or not. More than three-quarters of the buildings were gutted.

The discipline of the French soldiery and their allies broke down shortly after entering the suburbs and Moscow was given over to plunder and looting. The occupying troops often behaved badly to the remaining inhabitants, and there was a sharp increase in the numbers of Frenchmen murdered by civilians.

Napoleon, foolishly believing that the destruction of Moscow had strengthened his own bargaining power, sent two further messages to the Tsar in St Petersburg, asking for an end to hostilities. Alexander, although deeply depressed, remained obdurate and ignored the notes. For he had lost much popularity in Russia, not on account of the defeats or his unwillingness to treat with the enemy, but because of his earlier friendship and alliance with the French. Napoleon was not easily discouraged and on 5 October he sent General Lauriston, the former French Ambassador to St Petersburg, to parley with Kutuzov outside the lines in what was in effect no-man's-land. Kutuzov would have done so, but General Sir Robert Wilson, who was present, protested. And so Lauriston had to make his way to Kutuzov to deliver a note which was forwarded to the Tsar. Alexander's only reaction was a letter of censure to Kutuzov and Bennigsen, forbidding all contact with the enemy.

Meanwhile, as Wilson noted with satisfaction some days later, 'regiments of Don Cossacks continued to pour in. Such a reinforcement of cavalry was perhaps never equalled'. And they brought with them abundant supplies.

Kutuzov's decision to move off to the south of Moscow, instead of northwards to Tver from where he might cover the route to St Petersburg,

Left: a field officer of the Ekaterinoslavsky Cuirassiers in parade dress, 1814; right: a trooper of the Glukhovsky Cuirassiers in undress uniform, of a pattern which was to remain in use for over fifty years

turned out to be a masterly one. It was unexpected by the French. Moreover, Kutuzov secured easy access to the Tula armament works, the Don territories and the rich food-producing areas of the south. After moving towards Ryazan he turned sharply westwards and, after a few days' forced march, arrived at Tarutino on the Kaluga road in the area to the south-west of Moscow. There he was suitably poised to threaten the westward communications of the French. On 18 October Kutuzov surprised Murat in a sharp engagement near Tarutino, inflicting on him 4,000 casualties.

On that day Napoleon gave the order to evacuate Moscow and begin the homeward march.

There were neither shelter nor supplies in Moscow for the 100,000 troops of the Grand Army to winter in the city. Nor could Napoleon direct the affairs of state of his huge empire from this eastern outpost. So admitting failure, he decided to return, using a more southerly route on which, he hoped, supplies might be available.

The French imperial forces moved south-westwards down the Moscow–Kaluga road but their progress was barred by a Russian force in Maloyaroslavets, and the fighting which followed was of such intensity as to discourage Napoleon from following the southern route. He then turned back northwards along the Smolensk road, the axis along which he had come, a route which had been eaten bare of all supplies thirty miles to the north and south.

Wilson, much encouraged by the Russian defence at Maloyaroslavets, exhorted Kutuzov to fall on the marching French columns and destroy Napoleon between Vyazma and Smolensk. But Kutuzov, acting either according to his own inclinations or to political instructions from St Petersburg, would have none of it. For he told Wilson that 'the destruction of Napoleon and his army would be of no benefit to Russia or to the rest of the European continent . . . only Britain would benefit'. This was a rather roundabout way of saying that it was in Russia's interest to preserve its own armies, the better to be represented at the final peace. Henceforth Kutuzov was shortly to hand over the conduct of operations to Platov

Trooper and officer from His Majesty's Cuirassier Regiment, c. 1801

The Cossacks were particularly daring and troublesome and it was dangerous to leave the highway in search of shelter or food. Scores of partisan bands raided and butchered isolated detachments. Terrible atrocities took place, the sight of which so sickened Wilson that he felt compelled to protest to the Tsar. Yet the French themselves were by no means guiltless and Russian soldier prisoners were done to death in their thousands when they could no longer be fed or guarded.

At the beginning of November Napoleon reached Smolensk, where Victor's reserve army held the reinforcements and stores. The withdrawing columns had already been reduced to 40,000 men. Even so the stores were not sufficient, for the undisciplined mass of soldiery plundered the depots, emptying the base in a few days. The bitter cold sapped the French strength and in the further battles about Krasny Napoleon suffered more serious losses. When the Grand Army fell back on the Berezina it was scarcely 20,000 strong.

Meanwhile, on the far northern flank, Wittgenstein's corps attacked Macdonald near Polotsk, drove him back to the south-west, and took the French military base at Vitebsk. In the south Admiral Chichagov had marched from Moravia and, joining up with Tormazov, moved northwards, seizing the great French supply base at Minsk. Chichagov then attempted to cut off the withdrawal route of Napoleon's centre column by occupying the crossing-places on the Berezina at Borisov. From the third week of November onwards the Russian Army began seriously to dispute French movement, Wittgenstein and Chichagov doing their utmost to destroy the remnants of those troops who had withdrawn from Moscow. But Kutuzov, impervious to Wilson's anger, displayed his customary inertia in failing to come to the support of his countrymen, excusing himself on the grounds that Napoleon's forces were still formidable and that it was foolish to risk defeat when cold and hunger would finish off the Frenchmen anyway.

In the event, this is what happened. The weather suddenly became colder. Wittgenstein and Chichagov, unsupported by Kutuzov, were unable to drive in Victor's rearguards, but cold

and his Don Cossacks, a cheap and easily replaceable source of soldiers. Kutuzov was content that his regular forces should make flank marches, doing little more than shepherding the enemy out of Russia. Wisely, he fought only when it suited him.

The Destruction of the Grand Army

When the spearhead of the Grand Army left Moscow it was 100,000 strong. Except for that of the guard, discipline had already been eroded by the loss of good leaders and, more particularly, by the demoralizing effect of looting and excesses. Caravans of plunder were included in the withdrawing columns. Very soon there was a shortage of food which could only be met by slaughtering draught animals. The heavy autumn rains turned the roads into a morass, in which animals foundered and artillery and carts had to be abandoned.

Officer and trumpeter-major of the Odessa Hussars, c. 1803

Grenadiers of the Liflyandsky Inspectorate of the Tavrichesky Grenadier Regiment, c. 1805

and panic destroyed most of Napoleon's forces and camp-followers waiting to cross the Berezina. Napoleon left for Paris.

In all about 400,000 of the original half-million-strong Grand Army failed to return from Russia. Russian losses were probably in the region of a quarter of a million.

The End of the Napoleonic Wars

Kutuzov, true to his nature, was disinclined to pursue the French beyond the Russian borders. Alexander, however, insisted that Russian forces should enter Germany, for the Tsar had come to look upon himself as the saviour of Europe.

In December 1812 Yorck's Prussian troops, without authority from the King of Prussia, went over from Macdonald's French corps to the Russians. Prussia welcomed the entry of Russian troops as liberators from the French yoke. The

timid monarch Frederick William was forced to follow and, in the following March, declared war on France. Kutuzov took command of a Russo-Prussian army, until his death in April, when he was succeeded by Wittgenstein. Only western Germany and the Rhineland remained to Napoleon.

By April, however, Napoleon had taken to the field again. At the beginning of May he won Lützen, driving Russians and Prussians back behind the Elbe. Three weeks later he defeated them again at Bautzen, but this time the Russians yielded the field in good order and were shortly ready for battle once more. Wittgenstein lost his command to Barclay de Tolly.

Austria meanwhile used its good offices to attempt to arrive at a peace settlement. Napoleon was willing to talk, since every day gained strengthened his position. By August it was apparent that Napoleon was disinclined for peace, except on his terms, and war was resumed, Austria joined Russia and Prussia.

Napoleon won the two-day battle of Dresden, but a few days later Barclay won a victory at

Kulm. In October all three allies converged on Leipzig for the 'Battle of the Nations', on which field, between 16 and 18 October, Napoleon was decisively defeated.

On 30 March 1814 Alexander entered Paris. Napoleon abdicated on 11 April and was exiled to Elba. In the final three-day campaign in 1815, which culminated in the Battle of Waterloo and the end of Napoleon, neither Russian nor Austrian troops took part.

NOTES

1. In 1790 the field organization of the Russian Army stood at:

50 REGIMENTS OF CAVALRY

Horse Guards	1	Cuirassiers	5
Horse Grenadiers	1	Carabineers	13
Horse-Eger	2	Hussars	14
Dragoons	14	Cossacks	6

208 BATTALIONS OF INFANTRY

Guard Regiments	3	Eger Corps	10
Grenadier Regiments	13	Corps Battalions	22
Fusilier Regiments	56		

2. In 1812 before the recommencement of the war the 170 regiments of field infantry were made up of six guard regiments; fourteen grenadier regiments; ninety-six fusilier regiments; fifty light infantry regiments (not necessarily rifle-armed *eger*; four marine regiments.
(First-line infantry numbered in all 286,000 men.)

3. The seventy Russian cavalry regiments comprised six guard regiments: Gentlemen of the Guard; Horse Guards; Hussars; Dragoons; Lancers; and Cossacks (all the guard regiments had five squadrons except for the Cossacks which had three); and sixty-four cavalry of the line regiments: eight cuirassiers regiments; thirty-six dragoon regiments; eleven hussar regiments; five lancer regiments; and four Ukrainian Cossack regiments. (Line regiments had five squadrons except for the hussars and lancers which had ten and Ukrainian Cossacks which had eight.)

4. Since 1806 the artillery brigade had been taken into use. The 1812 Russian artillery strength was: Guard, one brigade of two horse batteries and four foot companies; Line, twenty-seven brigades of three companies; ten reserve brigades of four companies; four depot brigades of eight companies.

5. The deployment of Russian troops in the west in May 1812 (including a number of Cossack regiments called up from the hosts):

1 ARMY (BARCLAY DE TOLLY)

CORPS	Inf.	Cav.	Cossack
Infantry	*Bn*	*Sqns*	*Regts*
1 Wittgenstein	28	16	3
2 Baggovut	24	8	
3 Tuchkov	24	4	1
4 Shuvalov	23	8	
5 Constantine	27	20	
6 Dokhturov	24	8	
Cavalry			
1 Uvarov		20	
2 Korf		24	
3 Pahlen		24	
Platov			14

2 ARMY (BAGRATION)

CORPS	Inf.	Cav.	Cossack
Infantry	*Bns*	*Sqns*	*Regts*
7 Raevsky	24	8	
8 Borosdin	22	20	
Cavalry			
4 Sievers		24	
Ilovaisky			9

3 ARMY (TORMAZOV)

CORPS	Inf.	Cav.	Cassack
Infantry	*Bns*	*Sqns*	*Regts*
Kamensky	12	8	
Markov	24	8	
Sakken (depot corps)	12	24	
Cavalry			
Lambert		36	9

Trooper in undress and non-commissioned officer in everday uniform of His Majesty's Cuirassier Guards, c. 1803

The Plates

A Ryadovoi (Trooper) of the Guards Cavalry Corps, in everyday uniform, 1799–1800

The guards cavalry was re-formed in April 1799 into a composite guards cavalry corps under the auspices of the Grand Master of the Order of St John of Jerusalem, and the Cross of St John was incorporated into the intricate cap-badge. The corps was designed to fill the very pressing need for light cavalry and the troopers were armed with the 1797-pattern broadsword, a pair of pistols carried one each side in the pommel holsters of pig-leather (and known for this reason as *chushki* or pigs), and a carbine carried on the right-hand side and suspended by a swivel to the broad shoulder-belt of Russian red *yuft* leather running over the trooper's left shoulder. The soldier carried the sabretache (*lyadunka*) commonly worn at that time by sword-carrying infantry as well as cavalry: the sabretache, like the *porte-épée*, and scabbard being in red moroccan leather, trimmed at the edges with raspberry-coloured silk and carrying on it a brass and silver star with the Order of the Cross. The horse is ridden, as with all guards cavalry, on the curb rein of the rather fierce long-cheeked Pelham bit, the lower chain visible in the drawing being an ornament and not the curb chain which fits, of course, closely under the horse's chin. The uniform insignia is of particular interest, since its introduction commemorated the assumption by the Tsar Paul I of the Grand Mastership of the Maltese Order of St John.

B1 Fusilier of the Kievsky Grenadier Regiment, winter field service uniform, 1797–1801

The design of this uniform, which was in general use at about this time, was taken from that of the Gatchina infantry. The tunic (known as the *caftan* or *mundir*) was in the dark green colour traditional to the Imperial forces, and the pattern was not

31

Insignia of rank (full dress) of a general; right: a general-adjutant, cuff and collar facings, 1808 and 1815

very different from that worn by the infantry of the Empress Catherine II. There were variations by regiments; some wore white metal buttons and different-coloured facings; some Moskovsky regiments wore the parallel cuff woollen braid vertically instead of horizontally; but in the main the general appearance for the line infantry tunic was not greatly different. Underneath the tunic the soldier wore a red neckerchief, a shirt or waistcoat of the same colour as the pantaloons, usually white but in some regiments citron or straw-coloured, and in cold weather a sheepskin half-jacket or *shuba*. Pantaloons were of wool in winter and linen in summer and the spats or leggings were of strong, black, canvas-like cloth. All the leather equipment for the soldier's accoutrements was of Russian *yuft* except for the pack which was of black calf-leather. The crossed white shoulder-straps were traditional to the Russian Army for nearly 150 years. The cap was of a very old-fashioned pattern since discarded in western Europe, with a thin metal covering bearing a crown, the inscription 'God is with us', and a large Imperial eagle. The musket was of

Prussian design, having a walnut butt and stock, brass and steel fittings with bayonet cleaning-rod and ramrod attached. In length it was one *arshin* fourteen *vershkov* (about fifty-two inches) or, with bayonet fixed, sixty-eight inches. It was inaccurate and had an effective range of less than 200 yards. The soldier carried a sword as well as a bayonet and a grey unlined winter greatcoat.

B2 Nestroevoi Serzhant (Non-combatant Sergeant) of an Infantry Regiment, walking-out dress, 1786–96
Non-combatant officials formed a considerable part of the Tsarist Army and carried out a wide variety of functions. They manned the supply and transport service both inside and outside the regiments; they were the collectors of the wounded and what passed in those days for the medical orderlies, known as overseers (*nadzirateli*) of the wounded; they were the commissariat and the sutlers, the clerks, the draughtsmen, the artisans, and even the barbers; some were officials of officer grade, doctors, surgeons, auditors, pay-

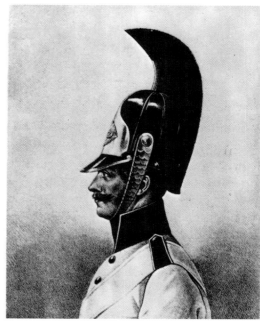

Cavalry head-dress 1803–8. Left: a curassier trooper and non-commissioned officer; right: a non-commissioned officer of the Grebensky Cuirassiers

masters, apothecaries, and priests. For the other ranks, the pattern of the uniform was similar to that shown here, always in green with the red cap, wearing the *tesak* sword and a cane for the walking-out dress. Although they were classified as non-combatants, they carried a musket or pistol in time of war. Non-combatant officials of officer grade wore the everyday green officer's uniform, but their swords were of a distinctive pattern with a straight blade and a single guard on the hilt.

B3 A St Petersburg Grenadier, winter general service uniform, 1808

By a new army regulation of 7 November 1807 all heavy infantry, that is to say line and grenadiers, were to have distinguishing patches on the greatcoat collar and the tunic collar and cuffs, denoting the seniority of each regiment in the division: red for the first, white for the second, yellow for the third, dark green with thin red piping for the fourth, and sky-blue for the fifth.

In addition grenadier regiments were to wear a distinctive colour on the shoulder-straps (*pogoni*): yellow for St Petersburg, white for Siberia, and red for the remainder, the number of the division, where applicable, being shown on the grenadier's shoulder-strap, in gold for officers and stitched for other ranks. The new pattern of uniform showed French Napoleonic and Prussian influences and was to remain in service, little altered, for the next forty years. The greatcoat, carried rolled over the shoulder in traditional fashion, was grey, the winter woollen pantaloons being exchanged in summer for those of Flemish linen. At his back the grenadier carried a sword and bayonet scabbard, a black leather *lyadunka* or cartridge-case bearing the same regimental crest (the flaming grenades) as was worn on the cap, a black calf-leather pack and a water-bottle. The regulation load for the pack was two spare shirts, one pair pantaloons, footwrappings (instead of socks), a soft forage-cap, spare boots, drawers, twelve flints for the flintlock, three brushes, two graters, a button-stick, pipeclay and boot polish, and a housewife. The summer weight of the pack was 25 lb, in winter 26½ lb.

A non-commissioned and a company officer of the Moskovsky Grenadiers, c. 1801

C1 Officer of Horse Artillery, summer general service uniform, 1797–1801

The artillery had not long before been accepted as an arm of the field army rather than as auxiliaries, and the pattern of the uniform at this time showed the officer to be more like a country squire than a soldier. No epaulettes or badges were worn and there was little about the wearer, except for his straight and heavy cuirassier officer-pattern sword to show that he was part of the Tsar's regular forces. Mounted, of course, he looked a little more imposing, usually on a bay charger with a dark green gilt-edged shabrack with the Emperor's monogram surmounted by a crown embroidered in gold in the corner and on the holster covers. The uniform of the horse artillery at the time was almost identical to that of foot artillery, but, by 1812, the horse artillery adopted a pattern of dress very like that of cuirassiers and dragoons with a high-crested tall helmet, a short green tunic with a black high collar and cuffs edged in red, red and gold epaulettes, a white cummerbund, and grey trousers buttoned at the side from hip to ankle bone.

C2 Infantry General, summer parade uniform, 1808–10

The commanders of all formations of the size of brigade and above were part of the *generalitet*, another military collective borrowed from Prussia, although in the guard regimental commanders might be major-generals. Generals were usually classified, again German fashion, according to arm so that as full generals they were known as Generals of Infantry or Artillery. The pattern of the collar and sleeve braid was usually common to arms, however, except that the *General-Adjutant* a designation bestowed also on admirals (who shared the army ranking system), had his own very distinctive gold braid pattern.

C3 Unter-Ofitser (Junior Non-Commissioned Officer or Corporal) of the Sumsky Hussars, summer parade dress, 1797–1801

The Sumsky Hussars claimed that they were one of the oldest regiments, if not the oldest, in the Imperial Army, having been founded, according to tradition, in 1651 as the town Cossacks of the frontier town of Sumy, near the Russo-Ukrainian border about half-way between Kiev and Kharkov. These town Cossacks were in fact regular forces and had no connection with the main Cossack hosts, and during their long life the Sumsky cavalry had been Cossacks, dragoons, uhlans, and hussars. But even among hussars they were regarded as an aristocratic and exclusive regiment and the regiment was often included in the guard cavalry corps. In winter a blue-grey cloak with fawn fur edging was worn, together with heavier brick-red breeches with a white stripe at the edge. The long flowing shabrack saddle-blanket was blue-grey with white toothed edging, and bearing the monarch's monogram at the rear.

D1 Bombardir (Bombardier) of Foot Artillery, summer field service uniform, 1808–9

A *bombardir* was later, like his British equivalent, a corporal of artillery, but at this time he was a private of artillery, a gunner, usually manning a mortar or howitzer. Except that he carried no

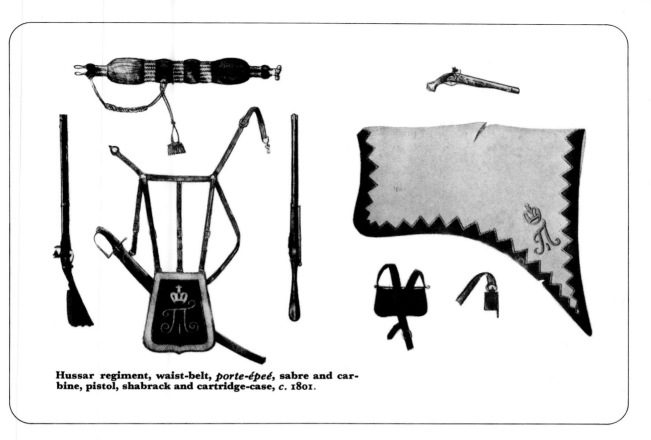

Hussar regiment, waist-belt, *porte-épeé*, sabre and carbine, pistol, shabrack and cartridge-case, *c.* 1801.

musket his equipment and his load were the same as that for an infantryman. Across his shoulder he slung his greatcoat, and on his back he wore a black calf-leather pack and water-bottle, a black *lyadunka* ammunition case, and the *tesak*, a straight-bladed short sword. He appears to have carried no other weapons, for French reports described Russian gunners defending their guns against cavalry and infantry, using swords, rammers, and handspikes.

D2 Unter-Ofitser (Corporal) of 8 Eger Regiment, winter parade uniform, 1802

Light infantry of foot (*eger* from German *Jäger*) usually wore a light green uniform, but the colour of the collar and sleeve varied according to the number of the regiment. *Eger* never wore the coloured shoulder-straps (*pogoni*) as did the infantry and the other arms. The greatcoat was of regulation grey, without shoulder-straps, and in summer all ranks wore white trousers of unbleached linen. Some regiments wore coloured piping on the green pantaloons. As light infantry their parade and skirmishing order was without pack and other impedimenta, no sword was carried other than a sword-bayonet similar to that in use elsewhere a century later. The firearm was a short-barrelled flintlock with an eight-groove rifled bore, the bayonet mounting being on the right-hand side of the barrel. This rifle was first manufactured as early as 1775. *Eger* rifle battalions provided the skirmishers and screens, relying on their fleetness of foot and long-range fire, to cover the main body of infantry and artillery.

D3 Ryadovoi (Trooper) of Uhlans (His Royal Highness the Tsarevich Konstantin Pavlovich's Regiment), undress uniform, 1803–6

Uhlans were light cavalrymen, armed with lance, sword, and carbine, first used by the Turks and then by the Poles in the Austrian service. Their name in Turkish meant 'children', and can be

Left: an officer of the Taganrog Dragoons; right: a hussar's head-dress, 1803

compared with the Italian *infante* in infantry. Uhlans were adopted by Austrian, Pole, German, and Russian. The honorary Colonel of the regiment, the Tsarevich Konstantin, son of the Tsar Paul and brother of Alexander I, had taken up his residence in Warsaw where he was a great admirer of Polish troops and Polish women. This trooper is shown in undress, wearing the soft forage-cap of the period. The dress for ceremonial parades was similar except that the forage-cap was replaced by the tall square uhlan shako, with glazed peak and high plume, and the blue overalls by dark grey pantaloons buttoned at the side from hip to ankle. The usual two broad white leather shoulder-belts were worn, one on each shoulder and crossing at the chest, one for the sword and the other for the carbine.

E Litavrshchik (Kettle-drummer) of the Glukhovsky Cuirassiers, ceremonial parade uniform, 1802–3
The Glukhovsky Cuirassier Regiment was originally raised at Glukhov, a town in the north-east of the Ukraine. The kettle-drummer wore almost the same uniform as that of the staff-trumpeter; in some cuirassier regiments buttons and braid were in silver and not gold. Like all kettle-drummers, when the drums were in play, he controlled his horse by snaffle reins attached to the stirrup-irons. Like dismounted non-commissioned officers he also carried the long walking-out cane (*trost*).

F1 Konduktor (Conductor or Senior Non-Commissioned Officer) of the Engineer Corps, everyday uniform, 1812–16
The engineer corps, including sappers, miners, and pontoon troops, were really an offshoot of the foot artillery and their uniforms had much in common. The grenadiers and artillery used the flaming grenade or bomb as the regimental badge, and the engineer troops followed suit. The shako, except for slight differences in the badge and plume, was identical and the tunic was somewhat similar to that of foot artillery. The engineers, however, wore thick grey overalls in winter (white

linen in summer) with the protective button-up gaiters. All other ranks of engineers carried the short sword as a side-arm.

F2 Trooper of the Tartar Horse Regiment, winter field service uniform, 1803–6

Tartar cavalry often served as part of Cossack formations although it was, of course, in no way Cossack, and the Tartar uniform dress was a curious mixture of pattern. The Tartar trooper shown here is wearing a uhlan shako, but his shoulder-belt, sabretache (not visible), and *porte-épée* all of Russian red *yuft*, together with the sabre are of hussar pattern, except that they are without the usual white silk or wool edge trimming. This particular Tartar regiment was sometimes paired with a Lithuanian horse regiment which was similarly accoutred. The nine-foot lance was carried by a shoulder-sling when mounted, or held in the crook of the right arm when on dismounted guard duty. The white sling on the left shoulder is attached by a swivel to a carbine (behind the soldier's back).

F3 Unter-Ofitser (Corporal) of the Balaclava Greek Infantry Battalion, ceremonial dress, 1797–1830

There were a number of small Greek colonies on the Black Sea ports and Tsarist Russia gave refuge to fellow members of the Orthodox religion fleeing from the oppression of the Turk. Two Greek battalions had been formed, the first in the reign of the Empress Catherine II, really as an expression of Tsarist goodwill to the Greeks, and they were used mainly for guard duties. They were very colourful, but their arms and equipment were so obsolete that, when eventually they were committed to battle, they demanded modern Russian arms. But these, when received, were no improvement and caused the Greeks to mutiny. The uniform of officers was similar to that shown on the plate, except that the gold edging was much wider and gold buttons were worn; private soldiers, on the other hand, had no gold braid at all. The difference between the first and second battalions lay in the variation of colours between waistcoats, shirts, cuffs, and collars, in green, dark green, and red.

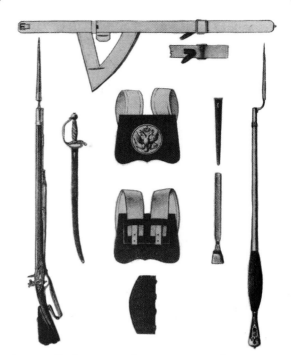

A grenadier's arms and equipment, c. 1801, showing musket with bayonet fixed, scabbard and lock-cover; *porte-épée*, short sword and cartridge-case

Insignia for General Staff (suite) officers in full-dress uniform, and (right) shabrack and holster-covers, c. 1808

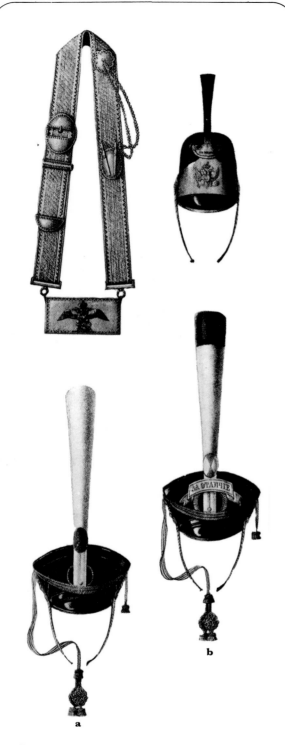

Top: a dragoon officer's cartridge-case and a shako of the Kiev Dragoons; below: the head-dress of the horse *eger* (a) trooper, (b) a non-commissioned officer, *c.* 1814

G1 Unter-Ofitser (Corporal) of 24 Eger Regiment, walking-out dress, 1806–7

There was some variation in the uniforms of the foot *eger* regiments. Most were in light green uniforms, but they could also be found, as here, in dark green tunics and dark green or summer white linen overalls. The collar and cuff colours were of course another distinguishing feature, which varied between regiments. All *eger* regiments were, however, armed with the rifled carbine and all wore black leather belts and accoutrements. Unlike the line, other ranks never carried the sword but relied on the bayonet as the side-arm. The newly introduced stove-pipe head-dress shown in the plate was common in other armies of western Europe. For fatigue wear or in undress the stove-pipe head-dress was replaced by the forage-cap with a drooping crown and hanging tassel, looking very much like the nineteenth-century nightcap.

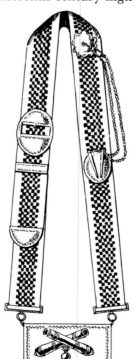

Horse artillery officer's cartridge-pouch and forage caps worn by other ranks of the garrison artillery, *c.* 1811–17

G2 Ober-Ofitser (Junior Officer) of the Kirnburnsky Dragoons, winter parade uniform, 1812–14

At about this time there was much change in the detail of the uniform of the cavalry of the line, for the Kirnburnsky Dragoons could also be found with brass spurs, and a light green tunic, usually

Left: a non-commissioned officer of the Tversky Dragoons; right: a *Fanenjunker* (officer aspirant) of the St Petersburg Dragoon Regiment, *c.* 1803

worn with the white cloth summer pantaloons. Each dragoon regiment was allotted a basic colour, although a single colour might be shared by several regiments, and this colour was common to the collar patch, the cuff, the shoulder-straps (*pogoni*) and the saddle-cloth.

G3 Ryadovoi (Trooper) of the Liflyandsky (Livonian) Horse-Eger Regiment, winter parade uniform, 1813–14

Whereas the dragoon was meant to be the mounted heavy infantryman, the horse *eger* filled the need for mounted rifles. Like his cousin of the foot he was the skirmisher and the scout, finding the screens and standing patrols for cavalry as well as infantry. Yet he was supposed to be able to fight as cavalry, for he carried the heavy-pattern curved cavalry sword. His uniform was something between that of the horse artillery and the dismounted *eger*, and at his back he carried a black leather sabretache surmounted by the Imperial double-headed spread-eagle in brass. His horse shabrack was in dark green edged in red.

H1 Bombardir of Horse Artillery, winter parade uniform, 1814–16

The horse artillery wore a distinctive head-dress quite different from that of the foot and carried the mounted-pattern sabre. Ranks could be distinguished by the horse-hair *sultan* or plume. A private soldier had a plume, as shown in this plate, of white with black and orange at the root; non-commissioned officer's was black and orange at the top and white below; a trumpeter's was red. An officer's was different again in design. Foreign spectators at about this time reported that the horse artillery also wore a uniform very similar to that of dragoons or cuirassiers, with the high fur combed helmet, a green tunic and grey overalls buttoned up at the side.

H2 Pontonier of a Pontoon Regiment, field service uniform, 1805–7

The Russian engineers, sappers and miners were, as we have said, an offshoot of the gunners and in 1805 the pontoon regiments were still listed under artillery. In consequence the uniform was little

39

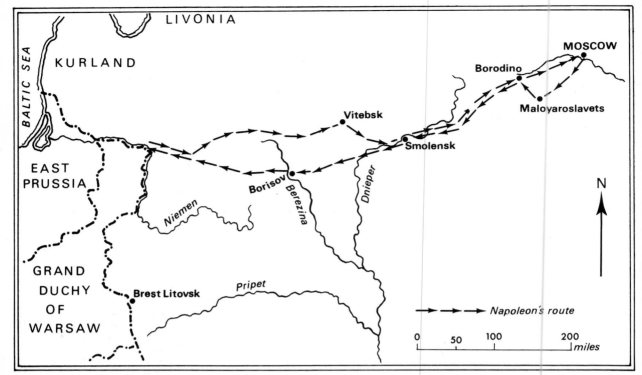

Napoleon's march on Moscow, 1812

different from that of the foot artillery, from which the pontonier could be distinguished only by his black shoulder-strap and the black cockade in the centre of the other ranks' shako. The pontonier could also be found wearing grey overalls, buttoned up at the side, instead of leather knee boots. The wide white leather shoulder-belt carried a black leather ammunition case displaying the Imperial double-headed spread-eagle in brass. The pontonier carried a curved half-sabre and not the foot-artilleryman's straight-edged *tesak*.

H3 Unter-Ofitser (Corporal) of Astrakhan Cuirassiers, winter ceremonial parade uniform, 1812–14

By a St Petersburg order of 12 October 1811 the Astrakhansky Cuirassier Regiment and the Novgorodsky Cuirassier Regiment were ordered to change the colour of their uniforms, the Astrakhansky Regiment taking a plain yellow uniform while the Novgorodsky Cuirassiers took pink. Otherwise the design of their uniforms, in common with most other cuirassier regiments, was almost identical except for the collar and shoulder-strap colours.